EAST ANGLIAN WORDSCAPES

EAST ANGLIAN WORDSCAPES

A Sequence of Twenty Poems
by
MERCER SIMPSON

with drawings by
MIRIAM KING

Rockingham Press

Published in 1993
by
The Rockingham Press
11 Musley Lane,
Ware, Herts
SG12 7EN

Copyright of the poems © Mercer Simpson, 1993
Copyright of the drawings © Miriam King, 1993

British Library Cataloguing-in-Publication Data

A catalogue record for this book
is available from the British Library

ISBN 1 873468 12 1

Printed in Great Britain
by Biddles Limited,
Guildford

Supported by the **Eastern Arts** Board

For the Old Burians,
and especially for
Michael and Margaret Forster

ACKNOWLEDGEMENTS

"Grimes Graves", and "Field Day on Cavenham Heath" first appeared in *New Prospects Poetry*. The latter poem was reprinted in *The Old Burian,* (the Old Boys' journal of King Edward VI School, Bury St. Edmunds) in which "Upon Ickworth House" and "Revisiting the Old School" made their debut. I am grateful to David Weston, the editor of *The Old Burian,* for the improvements he suggested to "Revisiting the Old School". I must also thank Margaret Harlin, Assistant Administrator of the Welsh Academy of Writers (English Section), for transferring my typescript onto disk at a most busy time. My final thanks are reserved for Miriam and Terry King for the journeys they undertook in the cause of art, and in particular Miriam for her sensitive interpretation of the poems.

Some people who no longer live in a particular place still carry it inside them, and speak from or through it even when they are not speaking about it.

Jeremy Hooker, "Living in Wales", *Poetry and Place* (Carcanet, 1982)

I always come back in the end to the things, the ground, the human scale of place, because the belief is rooted in me ... that the care of people for their place, which means their active care with and for others, is the foundation of human life.

Jeremy Hooker, "Barbarous Reflections" (12),
        The Presence of the Past (Poetry Wales Press, 1987)

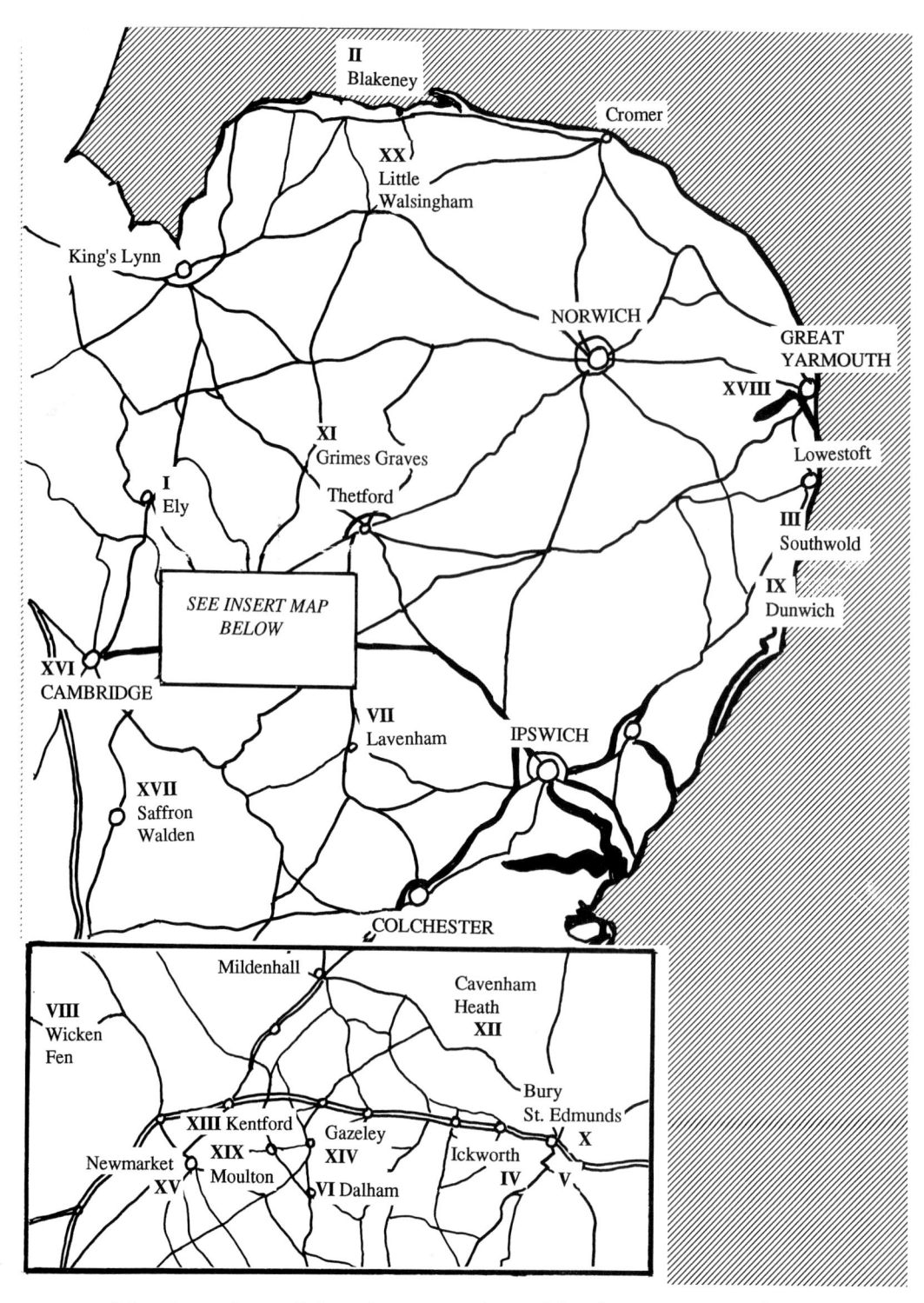

The location of the sites mentioned in the poems and illustrated by the drawings : each Roman numeral indicates a poem in the Contents list opposite.

CONTENTS

I	ELY CATHEDRAL : THE VOYAGE OUT	12
II	A POSTCARD FROM BLAKENEY	15
III	SEACOAST SOUTH OF SOUTHWOLD	17
IV	UPON ICKWORTH HOUSE	20
V	REVISITING THE OLD SCHOOL	24
VI	ST. MARY'S, DALHAM : EASTER AND OTHER SACRIFICES	27
VII	WOOL-GATHERING AT LAVENHAM	31
VIII	BIRD'S-EYE-VIEW, WICKEN FEN	33
IX	DUNWICH : THE LAST SURVIVOR	38
X	ON THE WEST FRONT, ST. EDMUNDSBURY ABBEY	42
XI	GRIMES GRAVES	45
XII	FIELD DAY ON CAVENHAM HEATH	47
XIII	GIPSY BOY'S GRAVE, NEWMARKET	50
XIV	HARVEST EVENSONG AT GAZELEY	54
XV	ON NEWMARKET HEATH	57
XVI	SUNLIGHT ON THE BACKS, CAMBRIDGE	59
XVII	TURF MAZE, SAFFRON WALDEN	61
XVIII	NOT FAR OFF BREYDON WATER	63
XIX	PACK-HORSE BRIDGE, MOULTON	66
XX	PILGRIMS TO WALSINGHAM	70
	NOTES ON THE POEMS	73

... the asymmetrical West Front,
opening out like a telescope,
reverberating skyward.

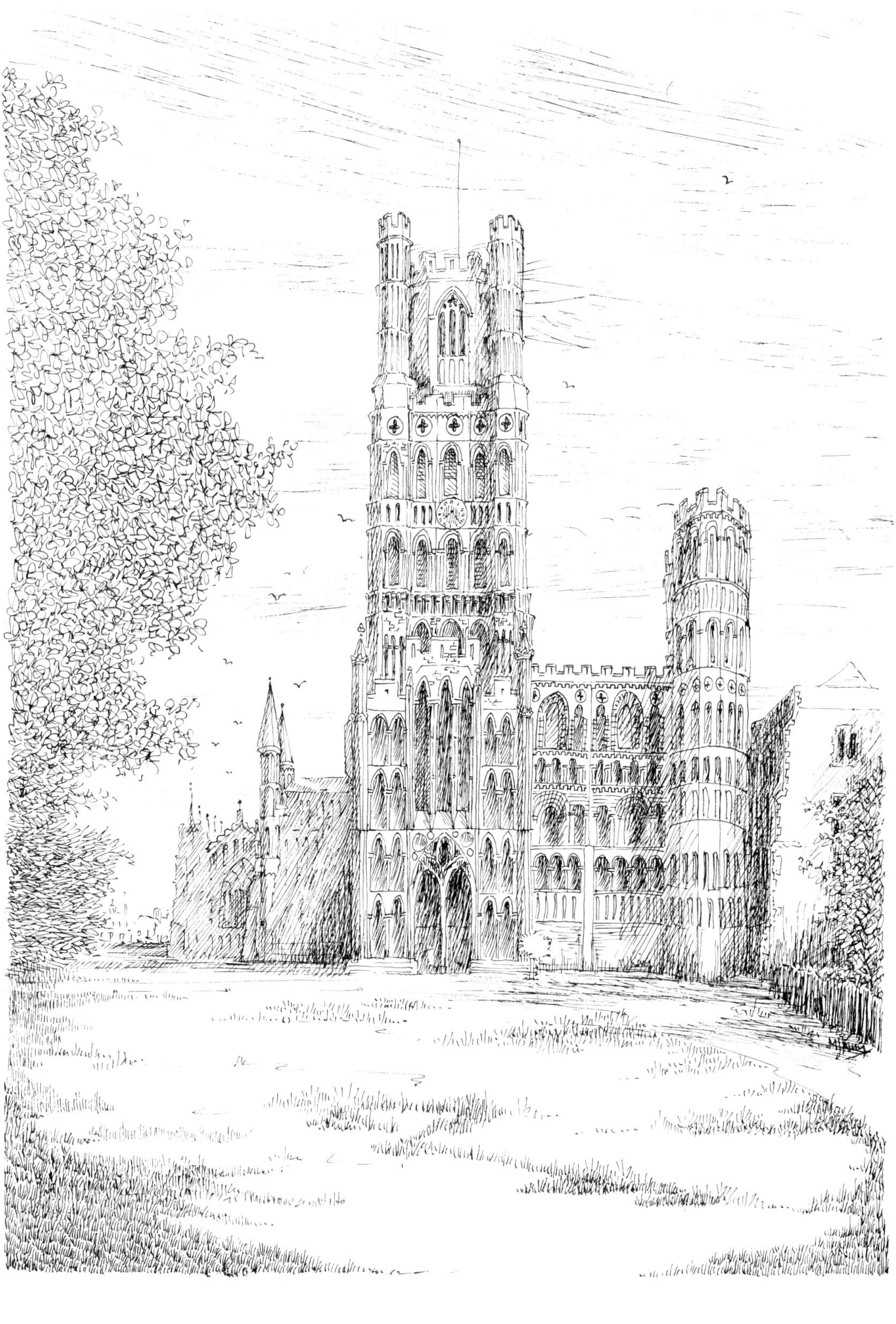

I   ELY CATHEDRAL: THE VOYAGE OUT

God's battleship moored off Stuntney,
your superstructure dominates
the Fen's grey sea.
Keeper of historical conscience
after Hereward, island of piety
on which the tower collapsed,
Alan of Walsingham's genius
then framed the crosstreed lantern,
octagonal control tower for Captain Christ,
beamed like a lighthouse to sweep the fields
where superstition froze in hard as turnips
among the misty levels of the huddled
cottages in villages
which kept low profiles.
Having refused to trawl the Wash
for a dilatory king's jewels
fishers of men being your priority
no ransom was too high lest you compromise
freedom of conscience, your body hull
racked out to an extraordinary length
three centuries on, surviving dissolution
with an abbot-bishop as the obligatory
thirty silver pieces from loyal townsfolk
outbid King Henry's agent. Necessary
as a fortress, no mere island sanctuary,
anchored beneath their swing of sky
towers move against swift clouds, reflect
a sunshaft's sudden dazzle on high windows,
an angel's wing carved in a secret arch
lost in the asymmetrical West Front,
opening out like a telescope,
reverberating skyward. Close up,
your power pins us aground in admiration,
idolators shipwrecked on your stone island.

Your presence is taller than any admonition,
your architecture of a moral superiority.
Surely your guns are trained on gambling crowds
of surefire losers on the Heath
above Newmarket. Perhaps your canonry
can't range the Cambridge colleges,
precursor that you claimed to be
in mediaeval learning. Too far to row
the training crew today. But if
you upped your anchor, moved off in the night,
made miracles from a gap in air
intensifying mist that swirled in from the Fens
with salvoes of learning long discharged
to cover your retreat, through such a gap
landscapes of disbelief confuse the lost,
as when the great tower fell. With mouths
as open as the graves at resurrection-time
we should look back to find the long-loved gone
and level land an open sea.

The fishermen have departed .../ Sloping masts point/ to the feared nor'-easter/ in a ceremony of hulks/ beyond redemption.

II A POSTCARD FROM BLAKENEY

Wrinkled horizons
doze with open eye
vague in sea's memory
and, save for springtide surge,
chained into mud,
have turned their backs upon the sun.
Far out, a sea wall
of unthreatened earth
gathers dunes sprouting marram
but swallowing footprints,
banishing low water mark
to an exiled horizon.
Only the ozone drifting in
reminds us of a sea-coast
sharpening the breath in a grey mist
to springclean cobbled houses
with their prim chintz.
The fishermen have departed
into the frames of sepia photographs,
their background abandoned gear and tackle.
Sloping masts point to
the feared nor'-easter
in a ceremony of hulks
beyond redemption.

This schoolboy bully gale/ brawls through the arches/
of ruined churches/ to peel off plaster from brick/
where the church shrinks into its tower/ at Walberswick ...

III SEACOAST SOUTH OF SOUTHWOLD

This schoolboy bully gale
brawls through the arches
of ruined churches
to peel off plaster from brick
where the church shrinks into its tower
at Walberswick
where this hooligan wind
has stripped the roof like a vandal.
On its way, it has shouldered aside
the ghost of Dunwich
far out to sea
with a drowned belfry
of tongues silenced by cliff-fall.
Through the spray's timeless explosion
interstices of mist
might recompose a coast
that's long departed.
Following the direction of invaders
that close eyes with dust,
mouths with sand,
hauls up its shroud from the east
to cover bones in the one direction
that time runs off the sea.
Do not speak against it
for your words will be blown away
off course into an inland meaning
of villages in soft green treelined hollows
and churches held in the hands of gentle hills.

... the giant rotunda, classical in symmetry

raising its head above the parkland and the walks,
the pillared portico, blind windows, as it mocks
the squat proportioned wings of Portland blocks.

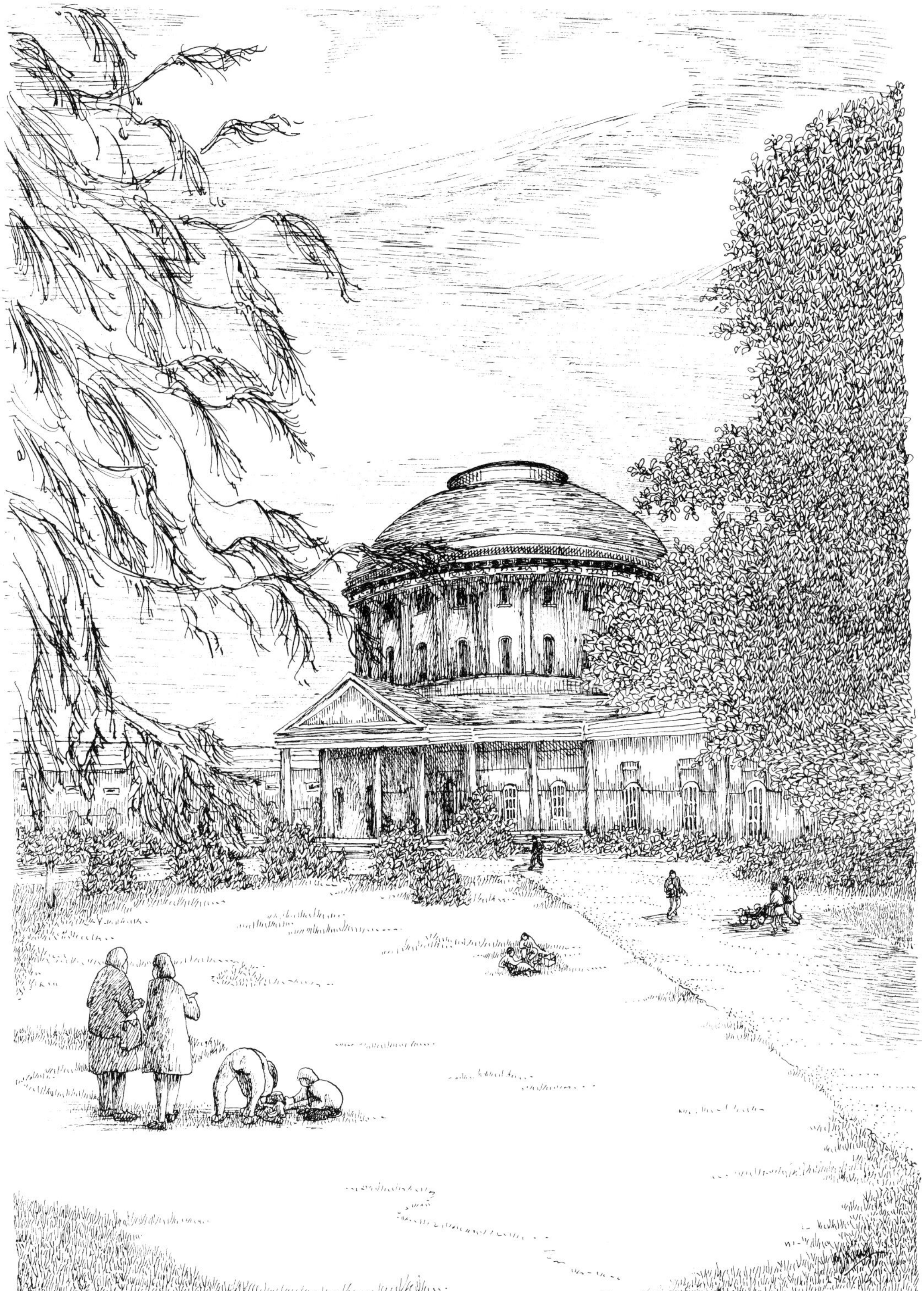

IV UPON ICKWORTH HOUSE

To house his pictures, which he lost in Italy,
the cleric duke built for his gallery
the giant rotunda, classical in symmetry

raising its head above the parkland and the walks,
the pillared portico, blind windows, as it mocks
the squat proportioned wings of Portland blocks.

* * * * *

That was the classical way
of looking at it, formal, precise, detached
and everything in its proper place,
especially the servants, reminding one
of polished surfaces, elegance and perfect manners.

But self-expression finds a way. Life gets out
on the loose sometimes. Why should one always have to
keep up appearances?   Power allied to wealth is
a natural breeding ground for eccentricities.

Gossip pursued a late marquess in his apparent dotage.
He'd dress up in patched tweeds, unshaven,
point curious visitors in the direction of the house,
mumble in Suffolk dialect something suitably ambiguous,
pocket a small tip and touch his cap
and then resume his pretence of hoeing
everlasting weeds in the gravel drive.

One would like to imagine them meeting him formally
disguised by cleanliness and a Savile Row suit
an hour later in the drawing room, at afternoon tea
hiding a smirk at their embarrassment, if recognition dawned.

He'd shoot off gruff opinions from a complaisant hearthrug :
The cost of running this estate's prohibitive.
Damn'd Government won't help. One's got to help oneself,
picking up muffins from a tarnished silver salver
but still a twinkle in his rheumy eye.

And all those pictures, statues, *objets d'art*
gathering dust in the long colonnades
death duties waiting in the wings.

Fling open shutters, throw up blinds,
let in the sunlight and The National Trust.
Visitors will pay to view the house and garden
and pay for the gardener to weed the drive.

But Big School's gone.   That late Victorian wing,
a skyline landmark, is a gap in air.
There two long dormitories filled two floors,
all windows barred, with Study Row below,
ground floor Big Schoolroom ...

            ... The Head's old house
is being redeveloped into flats,
its cupola without the bell,
windows no longer watching us.

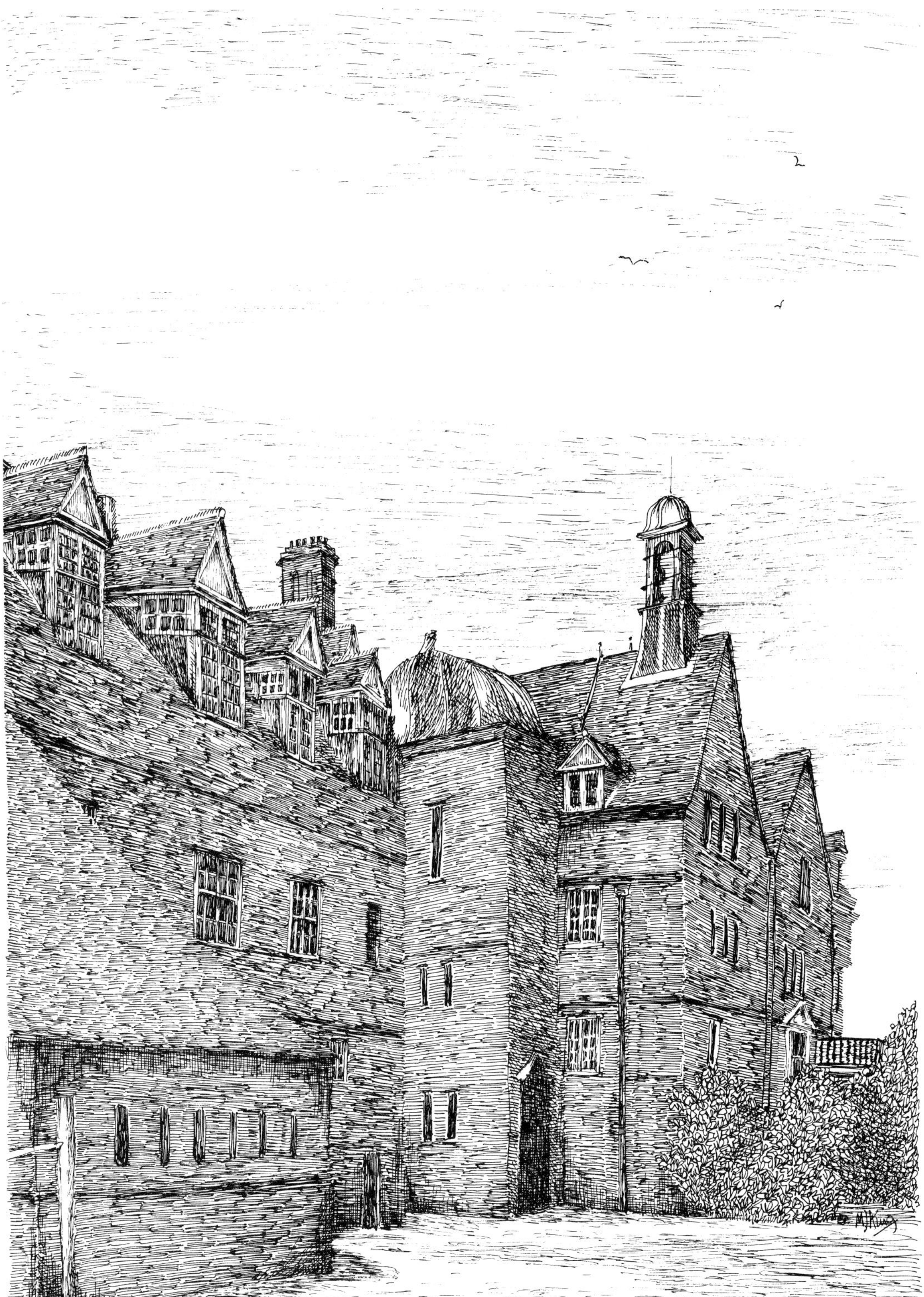

V REVISITING THE OLD SCHOOL

Odi et amo : quare id faciam, fortasse requiris,
Nescio, sed fieri sentio et excrucior.
(Catullus, *Carmina, lxxxv*)

Odi et amo ...
At the time, of course,
we hated it, but now the sharper memories
have blurred, some happiness remains,
something to do with being young again.
A half-remembered Latin tag :
Catullus, surely, but the rest won't come
and in a language that we rarely use,
that dies off into silence.

Faintest of echoes here about the place.
It's still a school,
but only now for juniors and girls.
New buildings and a swimming pool.
But Big School's gone. That Late Victorian wing,
a skyline landmark, is a gap in air.
There two long dormitories filled two floors,
all windows barred, with Study Row below,
ground floor Big Schoolroom, its long desks
almost from wall to wall, initials carved
throughout two centuries, looking down
between high windows, Honours Boards,
each name invisible among so many.
All who were there whether in gold leaf
or unofficial knife carved out their mark.
Beyond the Sixth Form Library, its books
bound with thick dust, four hundred years
accumulating from three sites ; perhaps
all knowledge comes to that, worth nothing more
but mixing with our own, into the cynic's vault;
a lack of it's a sweating palm,
the cane upraised, "adsum" replied to pain.

Not so today : staff cars
clutter a tarmac patch ; the caretaker
confided to us that he saved
Pro Patria Mori, World War I,
the cracked stone tablet stacked behind his shed
though couldn't resurrect these dead.
Even the Founder's bust was shattered in the dust
of demolition. The Head's old house
is being redeveloped into flats,
its cupola without the bell,
windows no longer watching us.
Beyond, the Playing Field's the same.
Some trees were felled and in the railway cutting
motorway traffic hums its way to Ipswich.
The green pavilion
still shelters in its trees, but the tense walk
out to the wicket doesn't seem so far
today ; failed adolescent heroics
aren't of importance any more
where only ghosts applaud.

Despite it all, we learnt some kindness here,
a modicum of learning but not much culture
small shopkeepers and farmers too close to nature
way off the road to Cambridge or to Durham.
A friend missed university, died in Burma;
I didn't know until I read his name
in the north aisle's memorial tablet
in the Cathedral.   Strange lottery
this life is, how we're all
shaken up in a gigantic box and then
flung out to scrabble for the prizes
and so forget to write and lose addresses,
moving on, side-stepping the obituaries.
So much experience hangs in the air
where people lived in buildings that have gone.
Only the sky is constant in its turn
when nights are truthful, clear and starry.
It's the immortal lie that makes us worry.

Their vault's unroofed now as the sky
a pocket of ruin long picked,
shaken and emptied against the nave's outside wall.

VI   ST. MARY'S, DALHAM :
EASTER AND OTHER SACRIFICES

The altar siting's
thirteen degrees off true:
its Saxon legacy's
magnetic north
lies in its foundations.

Shortly before the Civil War
the tower was rebuilt
by public subscription,
texts pricked out in flintstones
just below its battlements,
but the great gale
on the night Cromwell died
brought down its wooden spire.

Today, six months after our hurricane,
saws buzz and screech among toppled trees
in the woods screening the road
from village up to church and Hall.

Inside the church, a palimpsest
of murals peers through stripped plaster
and the devil leers down
from the north wall on a congregation
head down in prayer ; two acolytes
crouch under his wings. His arms
are like the branches of a tree,
knowledge of good and evil
for which God needs him.

So much for living in Eden,
enclosed by the tall walls of the Hall
gardens behind the churchyard :
who turned out the Afflecks

from their private vault
in the north aisle, scattering them
unceremoniously into separate graves
north side of the churchyard
with servants and labourers as bedfellows?
Their vault's unroofed now as the sky
a pocket of ruin long picked,
shaken and emptied against the nave's outside wall.
Their revenge : a great fungus
sprouted under the chancel,
prised up the tiles on the floor.
The resurrection of the dead
preserving grave mould
instead of the odour of sanctity,
death walking down the nave
without a wedding dress.
The smell's on the tiles still,
indelible white patches
the chill that shod our unrepentant
visiting feet. But their successors
remembered, outside, on the north wall
the loyalty of servants at the Hall
recorded on stone tablets. The Hall itself
foursquare, Queen Anne, looks over
the church's shoulder :
bonded together on the hill
gentry and parson count their tenants
climbing to Matins from the valley
like sheep into the hurdle-porch
of feudal custom, there put on
hairshirts of uncomplaining service.
They will be baptised with sheep-dip,
sent to the slaughter-house with absolution
pricked down as soldiers skewered in battle
and blinded with mustard-gas.
Bless you, my children:
the rector gives the sign of the cross
as they move to the right in threes,
rifles at the slope, bayonets fixed ;

out of step with history, they march away.
They will not be besieging Acre.
Jerusalem will never be built for them.

Passing downhill through the trees
that shroud the view of the village strung
along the stream like an imitation
pearl necklace of scattered beads,
they will be seeds in a casual wind.
They pass their shuttered cottages,
dissolve into a distance to become
grey wraiths of gunfire on the Somme.

Sermon for Easter - on the Crucifixion.

... the hunched, half-timbered shoulders of houses staggering into view like drunks after a night out leaning inward to support each other.

VII WOOL-GATHERING AT LAVENHAM

The massive uprightness of the tower
of the great church is a moral metaphor.
It presides above the devious intricacies
of streets escaping from its shadow,
the hunched, half-timbered shoulders of houses
staggering into view like drunks after a night out
leaning inward to support each other.
The flinty stare of the church tower
keeps all the records straight, fires off
broadsides of bells, once summoned to confession
the trickery of wool-merchants who built
this church for the profit of their consciences.
St. George's Cross on its flagpole
should keep out dragons : in the Guildhall Museum
history's sepia photographs expose
the burning of acres of myth, the ruts
that shattered axles and, standing aside,
the carefully posed profiles from the Hall,
the shooting party in their Norfolk jackets.
Down the green lane, the candles flicker under thatch
for cottagers whose looms warped out
trickles of yarn spun from calloused hands,
and slow-burning peat smouldered for generations
until an angry flame broke through.
Here England's first sugar-beet refinery
closed down through strikes before the end
of Queen Victoria's reign, fell into ruin
and the railway withered away to Sudbury.
The population's hardly grown in four hundred
years. Memory is sheep's wool
balled round barbed wire.

... we probe the secrecy of thickets,/ then emerge into revelations of/ cloud in a wind-stretched sky./   Along the long vistas/ windmill and warden's house/ keep reappearing/ with landmarks' reassurances.

VIII BIRD'S-EYE-VIEW, WICKEN FEN

Windthreshed reeds breathe in turbulence,
their whirlpool of tinnitus
the halfgale's pressure-cooker's
insistent hiss below the nod
and toss of treeheads. Up the hide's
steep ladders, we see no birds
but framed in a treegap, Ely's
West Tower's aflame,
diamond light in a sunshaft
catching our breath as we
prise open the creaking shutters
flying into the wind at the top
of a gently swaying wooden tower.
Below, on our walk, we record
two butterflies' heavywinged
reluctance for autumn,
and an infant grass-snake
with a yellow rectangle
like a leper's badge on the back
of its neck. At the end of the long
reach of dyke's whipped water
shaking its shoulders like a dog's,
a moored skiff peers out of
the quieter scumgreen beneath willow shadows.
East of the dyke, Adventurer's Fen's
a drained face : an artificial lake
where mallards huddle out of
fieldglass range, then spiralling away
above ploughland's expressionless stare.
Here, Wicken Fen's sleek gloss-green
haircut of sedge
cleaves smart direct partings :
dry springy paths in grid pattern
intersect shoulder-high grasses ;
keeping their distance,

tree sentries parade in rows
along their unattainable frontierposts
that belong to the sky.   Over the wetlands'
weaving of duckboard walks
a foot above the Fen,
thin slats taking on the spring of turf,
we probe the secrecy of thickets,
then emerge into revelations of cloud
in a wind-stretched sky.
Along the long vistas
windmill and warden's house
keep reappearing
with landmarks' reassurances.
We note the reeds' lessons
of thatch, the cottages'
roofs that sprung out of black mud,
how peat comes up in layers
like the uncut pages of history.
Whoever inherits this territory
will not speak directly to us
but will be looking back
anxiously over shoulders, into the trees
and at the fading light
behind branches, and listening.
Today we can hear nothing
above the wind in the reeds
whispering; incessantly,
insistently, whispering.
What we would know
is always just too far off.
Night's false scents laid,
the moon's suddenly cloudfretted,
staring back at us, a blurred
disc in greygreen pools.
Easy to lose one's way
and slide into the watery dark.
Here, even in daylight,
paths are for keeping to :
air and water for birds'
presence and absence.

Around the Fen, a sea of furrows,
wrinkled brown wavelets
speckled with gulls
break over a bird's eye view
of a secret island.
A stranger's eye, outside, at ground
even close up, might miss it.
Low, level land behind treelines
is territory for flying over,
for exploration looking down,
the birds' private kingdom
seen through a bird's eye.

But there's no hell-fire
in that curled-up corner awaiting
the sea's judgement ; under a solitary tombstone
the last survivor, John Brinkley Easey,
died 1826, aged only 23 ;
about to be reunited down below
with his former fellow-tenants of this ground,
going out, like them, feet first.

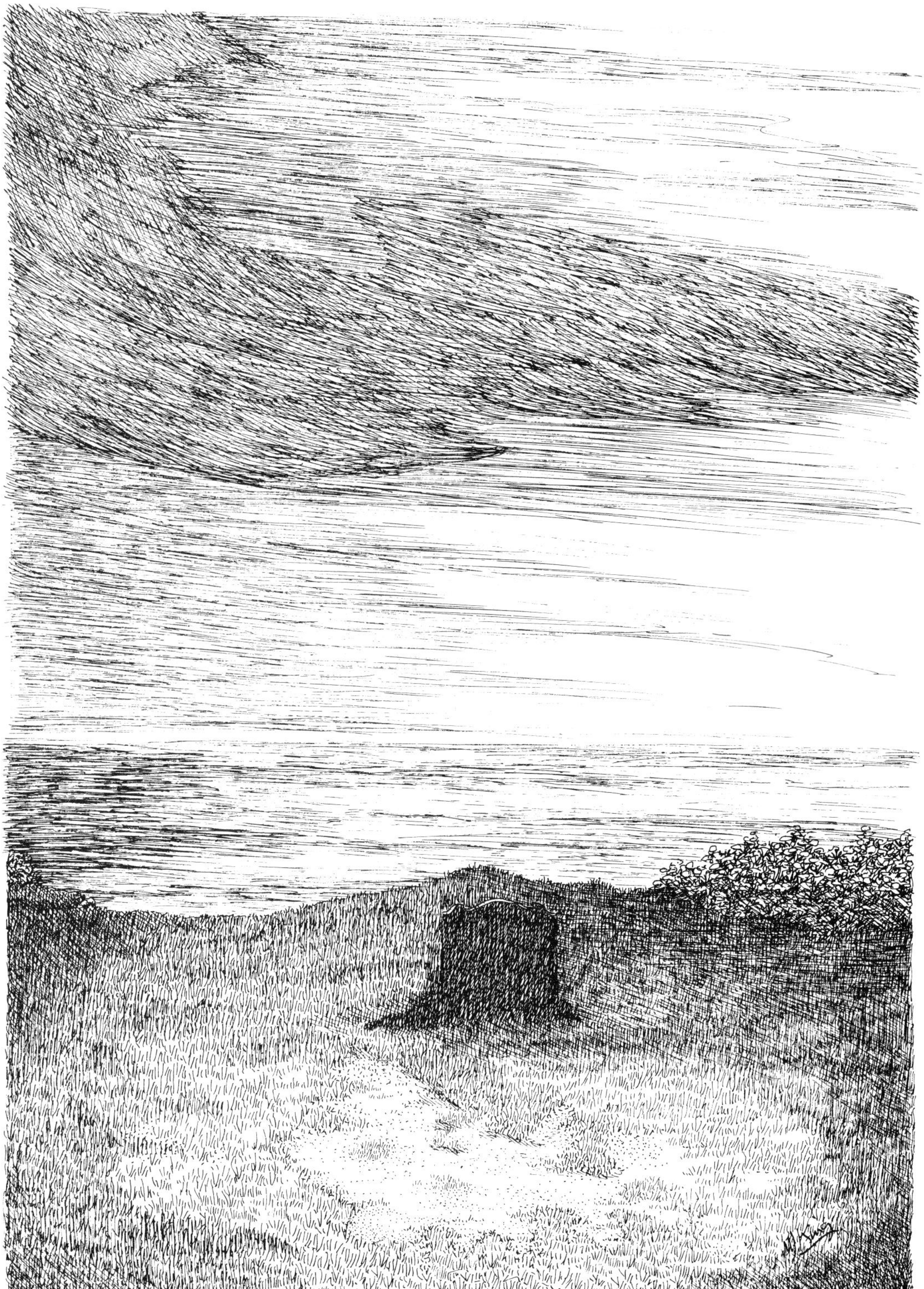

IX DUNWICH :
THE LAST SURVIVOR

All Saints', Dunwich: the town's last church,
in the middle of the eighteenth century
abandoned on the cliff after the final
inundation below, the last of the town
having been engulfed by a relentless
procession of storms; looking down on nothing
but the sea's curled wave-lip snarling at cliff's-foot,
the population all departed save those
in their exalted position in the churchyard.
They went on burying people there for another
seventy-five years; the church soon a ruin,
the chancel unroofed, stripped by the wind,
the tower's foundations undermined,
the windows open-mouthed, uncomprehending ;
but most of it's still standing in a late
Victorian sepia photograph,
the prospect smouldering away
until the bottom right-hand corner's all
that's left ; hold it too long and it will burn
your fingers. But there's no hell-fire
in that curled-up corner awaiting
the sea's judgement ; under a solitary tombstone
the last survivor, John Brinkley Easey,
died 1826, aged only 23 ;
about to be reunited down below
with his former fellow-tenants of this ground,
going out, like them, feet first. The bland
expressionless face under him is the cliff's
soft sand and gravel, pock-marked with flints.
The sea's mouth will suck at it.
Each coffin in its turn has been gnawed
by waves' rats'-teeth ; spilled out falanges first,
scoured out the rib-cage until the skull
was last to fall, found object seaweed-wreathed
upon the line of beach, ignominious
as driftwood at high-tide's scumline. Instead

there should have been sea-voices in the air above,
the shingle-grinding pebbly-mouthed ground-bass
for organ notes, both epilogue and elegy.
Dust of the drowned town's sluiced away
southwards under the scour of centuries
but still admixed with human dust :
the speck that sticks in a visitor's eye
wiped out with a handkerchief's corner
is a tear from a ghost. You, John, knew only
the story's ultimate chapter, almost to
the last word that's about to be written :
from your cliff-face you look out upon
erased pages, in grateful ignorance
unable to listen for history's laughter
gusting in the easterly gale
of He that is coming to promise your fall.
All in all, a long way from the resurrection
you might have been looking forward to.

Two hundred years on, after the Dissolution,
the Abbey Ruins flowered into houses,
time's colander holes in the West Front
patched up with reddish bricks, intruding lintels,
squared Georgian windows, rectangular tiled roofs
changing the expression in a dying face
until it came to life again, so that the Abbey's
now lost in it.

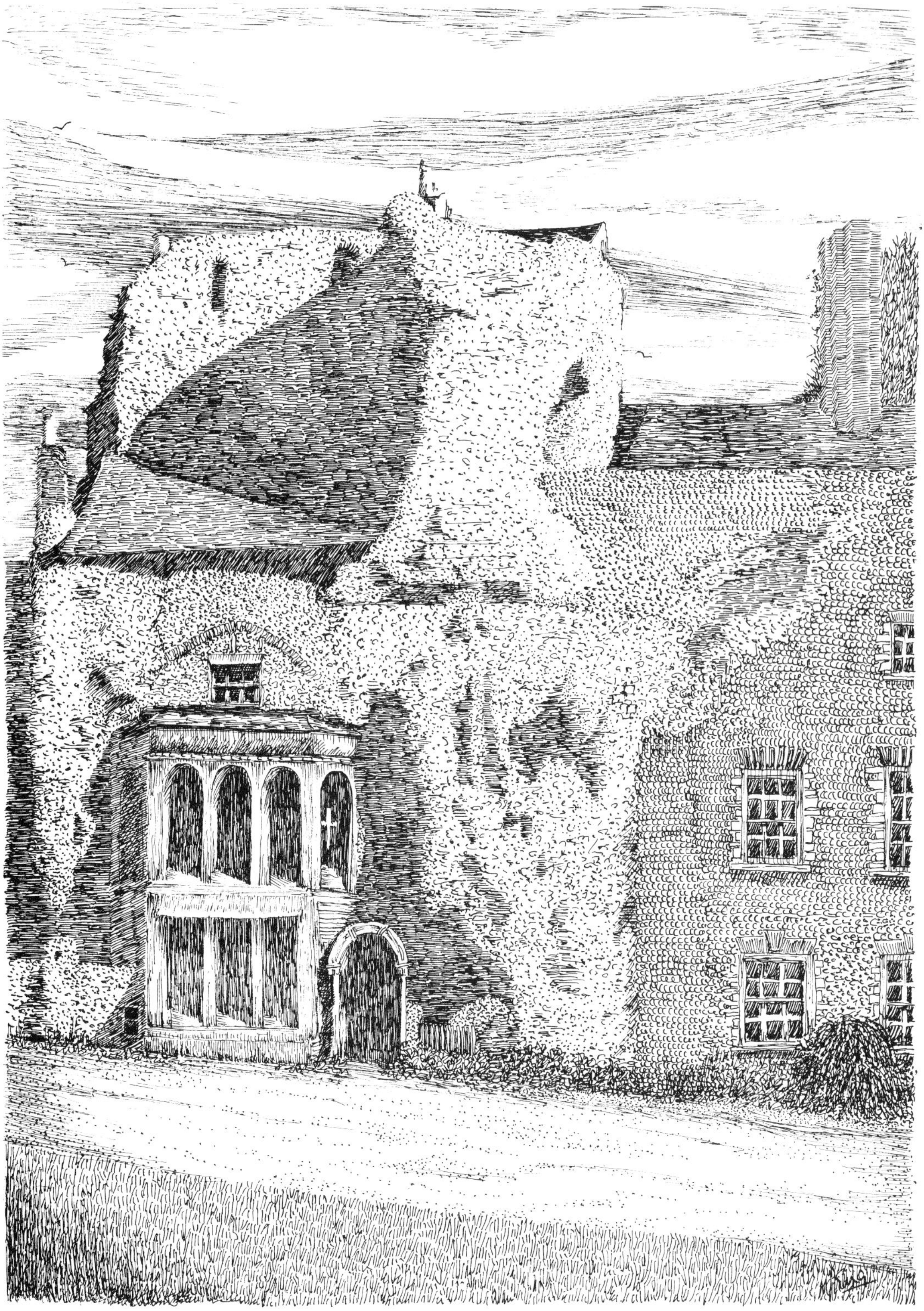

X   ON THE WEST FRONT, ST. EDMUNDSBURY ABBEY

Two hundred years on, after the Dissolution,
the Abbey Ruins flowered into houses,
time's colander holes in the West Front
patched up with reddish bricks, intruding lintels,
squared Georgian windows, rectangular tiled roofs
changing the expression in a dying face
until it came to life again, so that the Abbey's
now lost in it. This is how we repair
history in human terms, to bring it up to
a certain date, put ordinary people in,
help them to live out lives with a sufficiency
of comfort, secure behind great breadths of stone
like houses built out of caves in the vast
cliff-faces of the Dordogne. The facade's stone face
was holed as if by an artillery barrage
of townsfolks' hatred against the abbot's
exaction of tithes ; the building cowered
behind poisoned ivy ; but it never quite
came to burning, not for buildings here,
only for heretics, and later witches.
So if sometimes buildings look uncomfortable
in a changed and unfamiliar role
it's secular appetites imposing
violations on monastic tranquillity.
The stone face frowns in continuing witness.
Buildings become the people that have lived in them.
So do not worry if the Grey Lady
still walks across the rear lawns
which were once part of the Sanctuary ;
she too has her territorial rights
of suffering, she was dispossessed once
of house and love, for disobedience
of the rules of her nuns' order ; her lover,
almost certainly a monk, would have been
walled up somewhere behind that pained
and crumbling face of stone. Now, today,

they want to take away the houses,
turn out the people living in them,
rip them away from history, like a burnt
skin peeling off : to return to a gaunt
un-ivied ruin, hollowed out, a skull
with windowless sockets for its eyes,
all life gouged out.   But the nun will still walk.
She will pass through the deconstructed walls.
She will vanish into air at the precise
spot appointed for her martyrdom.
And the population of ghosts
will be what is left of human breath
on the stripped walls, its numbers increasing,
the stone, though whiter, remaining stained.
Acts of absolution are performed
only by those living in a place.

These small men's tunnels,
gnome-sized, aren't going anywhere.

XI GRIMES GRAVES

So names confuse a place's use.
Not the intention here for burial sites
even though neolithic miners
were buries alive in these bell-pits
whenever the roofs caved in.
Not much more than mere
holes in the ground, each one gouged out
by antler-picks' impatient scratchings at
soft walls that clasped flint-clusters'
hard cusps for hooking out
from a back-breaking angle.
These small men's tunnels,
gnome-sized, aren't going anywhere.
Out of their sweaty depths the first
walls grew above, foundations of
round houses in forest clearings.
Below, inside distorted echoes
voices are whispering
in a blurred, an incomplete
language. Above, on sandy soil
wind-tortured lines of Breckland firs
patrol the ridge ; sentries
nervous, alerted for the tribe's attack
coveting the sling-shot gold
sharper than treasure.
On a clear calm day
these voices climb into the trees
and rise into the sky like birds.

.... No sentries set./   All lying down, a couple half asleep./
Then from the copse, left, ten o'clock,/ less than a hundred yards, from
quivering undergrowth,/ the enemy came charging in, fixed bayonets.

XII   FIELD DAY
ON CAVENHAM HEATH

Cavenham, you said. *This was the place.*
O.T.C. Field day, Summer '43.
My puttees unwound themselves, inevitably,
so that I fell out on the long march there,
the blisters welling up in unfamiliar boots.
The sandy dust, the heat. Schoolboys
playing at soldiers, wearing uniforms that were
archaic, World War I. Brass buttons,
highly polished, down the tunic front.
No grease-paint faces, actors' camouflage.
No denims, battledress for World War II.
But we had rifles, carried blanks.
For unofficial bangs, our gleeful thanks.

Your section slumped down in the hollow
beside the River Lark. A lark indeed!
Tom Squires drew at his usual cigarette.
Fifteen minutes before the off. No sentries set.
All lying down, a couple half asleep.
Then from the copse, left, ten o'clock,
less than a hundred yards, from quivering undergrowth,
the enemy came charging in, fixed bayonets.

Ten seconds and the ambush was complete.
Your rival sergeant, so you claimed, had been a cheat,
attacking fifteen minutes early. *But that's war,*
the C.O., Captain Swainston, said.
And as we staggered to our feet
he, umpire, shouted out, *Lie down! You're dead, you're dead!*

Revisiting the site, we're glad we're still alive.
Called up too late to use these *Lessons of the War*
save on the parade ground, Depot R.M., Deal,
read Henry Reed on how the unmilitary survive.
Too young to shoot to kill, we can give thanks
for our war service, only firing blanks.

No one would notice it at the roadside
but for a surprise of flowers left by the sympathetic ones ...

49

XIII GIPSY BOY'S GRAVE, NEWMARKET

No one would notice it at the roadside
but for a surprise of flowers left by the sympathetic ones
who also put their shirt on love or life
believing the odds were evens.

You who placed your final bet, the longest shot
on the next world, might well be laughing at us
lacking the proof you didn't win.

Unrequited love for a rich man's daughter,
you a penniless gipsy boy, helping with the horses,
mucking out life's dung-spattered stables,
though straw's more comforting than sleeping out
under an alienated frostiness of stars
or the contemptuous stare of the moon
queening it over the Heath.

Found one morning with a bullet in your brain,
the stolen shot-gun conveniently beside you,
the verdict *Suicide, of unsound mind,* cliché
of life wasted, statistic for the moralists.

Hanged criminals were buried at crossroads
but why this site for you? Suicides usually
made it to consecrated ground, to the unfriendly
north side of churchyards where anonymous mounds
blotched shadows in the rustling night
through unkempt grass, uncared-for territory.

Yet on your wayside grave the flowers arrived.
No one would be seen to leave them there
but later on would find themselves some luck,
pick out the Guineas' long-odds winners,
run right through the card on the June Course,
the irony of winnings that you never had.

So myth grows, flowers, drops seeds
in the uncultivated zones beyond the norms
of calculations, averages, projections of
the actuarial chances ; the irrational
that brings a sense of wonder into life
is in the gambler's blood, the wayward hope
all will be happy in the end.
The primroses, bluebells, daisies, and forget-me-nots
share the copse's secret behind your grassy plot
and at night tiptoe out, encircling your grave
to dance around it, celebrating all the winners.

Behind a narrow screen of trees,
glimpsed through a macrocarpa tunnel-path,
in tombstone-pitted open ground,
large for the present village, Gazeley Church.

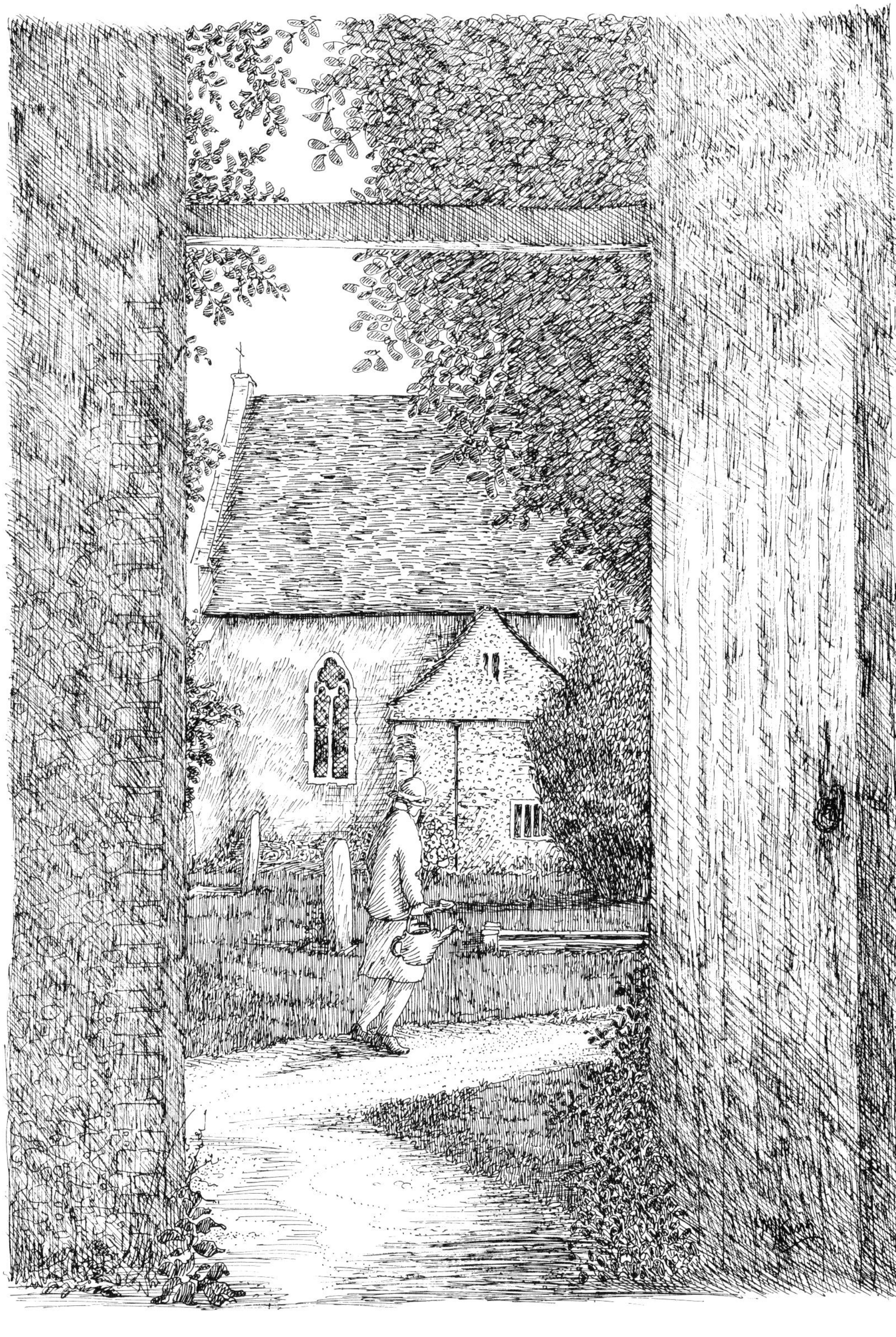

XIV HARVEST EVENSONG AT GAZELEY

A sweep of lawns, beyond tall trees,
Gazeley's Victorian rectory sleeps
behind its shutter-lidded eyes,
no tea-cup talk nor plock of croquet balls
from ladies prim beneath their parasols.
A hastily-erected fence divides
it from the modern rectory, untenanted
as yet ; no parish priest will be
inducted for some months.   Across the grass
blind houses staring helpless at each other.
This modern version's shrunk to functional,
not built for generous entertaining in.
Parked by the newly-painted door, moped,
skid-lid, a mackintosh and wellingtons
implying occupation, though the curtains
are all drawn. Behind a narrow screen of trees,
glimpsed through a macrocarpa tunnel-path,
in tombstone-pitted open ground,
large for the present village, Gazeley Church.
A sudden burst of organ practising.
My friend will take the Harvest Evensong.
The church is spacious and unspoilt,
unscarred by restoration.   Surprisingly,
the organ's at the back, behind the rows
of pews, wood-wormed and mediaeval-carved.
The organist is curly-haired, slim-featured,
her high-pitched voice as reedy as a child's.
At first glance in her twenties, then I see
she's nearer forty in unflattering light.
Sometimes the village life is harsh outdoors,
with North Sea gales that bite into the face,
setting there premature wrinkles, drying skin
to sunbrowned wheat, engaging ripeness here.
She travels round as organist, she says,
to all the neighbouring village churches.

And soon the congregation come in twos and threes,
the families with younger children too
until we have a hundred in the church.
Her organ playing's careful, ceremonious,
giving us time to linger over notes,
singing the louder joy and gratitude
for harvest and the gift of life
that runs more slowly here but happier.
The Sower got it right this time.
When I, a stranger, leave the church,
it's as though I'm going out with friends.
We all shake hands, talking as if we've known
each other years. This village friendliness
breaks bread of heaven, handing round the cup
from whose shared wine our happiness filled up.

A string of horses, jockeys in their silks,/ go cantering back to stables;/ trainer with stopwatch records a time,/ wonders who's watching from the woods/ that gather on the crest around the reservoir.

XV ON NEWMARKET HEATH

The thick grass is like a broomhead
but it's the winds that sweep across
invigorated space ; gallops for exercise
on artificial surfaces where tree bark shavings
ensure firm going when the rest is mud.
A string of horses, jockeys in their silks,
go cantering back to stables ;
trainer with stopwatch records a time,
wonders who's watching from the woods
that gather on the crest around the reservoir.
The sun rides full-tilt out of clouds,
lighting a field, and then one further off,
in nervous point-to-point towards the north,
the fens, the autumn bonfires' smudge
where stubble-burning's over, and the beet
will soon be harvested from fertile soil
drained from the levels of the dykes and reeds.
Ely Cathedral's lantern's silhouette's
a shadowy finger pointing heavenwards
reminding us that gambling is a sin.
In the Pepys Library at Magdalene,
far off in Cambridgeshire, betting slips
in the diarist's hand : *Five Guineas
with the Duke of York, the King won't leave
Newmarket for London tomorrow.*
I'd like to think Pepys won his wager ;
with commonsense, except with fillies,
he'd bet on certainties, never on horses.

The morning sun will melt The Wedding Cake,/ New Court, St. John's, that neo-Gothic fantasy,/ pure Beckford at a distance, closer up/ barred prison, stern, across a Bridge of Sighs.

XVI SUNLIGHT ON THE BACKS, CAMBRIDGE

Here all seems pointing to the sky,
reaching for knowledge — spires, crocketing,
decoration flamboyant as in rhetoric
or argument in theological dispute
as if God's up there looking down
to bless poor scholars, comfortable dons.
As eyes enthuse behind the spectacles
of lined owl-faces in dark libraries,
note-taking lecture rooms, they memorise the sun
glinting off buildings that float through trees
across the water on The Backs
in which the ripples break the mirror-images
at dip of punt-pole, eddying of swans
and flurries under bridges, secret currents
that whisper warnings to get back to books.
The morning sun will melt The Wedding Cake,
New Court, St. John's, that neo-Gothic fantasy,
pure Beckford at a distance, closer up
barred prison, stern, across a Bridge of Sighs.
Some colleges retreat behind their sham facades,
trite metaphors for spurious scholarship.
I like my own place best, in Magdalene :
quiet, civilised, and not too many there
to find your friends, assume identity.
In the Pepys Library, the diarist's pages hid
behind an uncracked code for nearly a hundred years.
History's like that : we stand too close to read
clear sense to decode our cluttered times,
and like an Ibsen plot strip off
the onion-layers, contradictory
until there's nothing left and tears.
Best celebrate the sunlight while it's there,
resting our backs against the warmth of walls
in gratitude the past's still present here.

... this is a maze for the faery folk,
a miniature path for the dancer
treading on tiptoe through intricate dreams ...

XVII TURF MAZE, SAFFRON WALDEN

Ghost of a Green Man walks the maze
stepping with delicate footwork
the Morris figures, intricate patterns
left in the curvilinear grooves of the lines
pricked out in new brickwork over the ground.
I prefer hedges to lose myself in,
hugging green secrets, privet or box,
or in tall yew walks, adorned by neat topiary
of beasts looking down on a live labyrinth.
On the flat levels here the eyes are drawn down
to the straying feet lest one stumble or cheat ;
originally walked for wagers,
this is a maze for the faery folk,
a miniature path for the dancer
treading on tiptoe through intricate dreams,
not quite what it seems with one's eyes on the sky.
Accept this, then, as a folk-memory,
aide-memoire, computer, map of the paths
to outlying villages, ways in the dark
where the Green Man would lead by the hand
lost maidens through mist, children through marsh.
Tread carefully through this, your unremembered country.

Not far from woods with grey-leaved willows/ the huge flint Roman walls of Burgh/ square-shouldered and round-towered;/ no other signs of life but birds/ who rise like scatterings of seed.

XVIII NOT FAR OFF BREYDON WATER

Suddenly, as if out of a tree clump
a boat's sails appear
in the middle of a green field
and move on through the pasture,
the Freisians keeping their heads down
apparently taking no notice.
Further on, opening out
into sun-glinting, small-waved water,
our boat's progress a gentle throb of engines
past wake-washed banks fringed by thick reeds,
dry-throated, confidential whispers.
Here windmills aren't for grinding corn
but derelict pump-houses.
Not far from woods with grey-leaved willows
the huge flint Roman walls of Burgh
square-shouldered and round-towered ;
no other signs of life but birds
who rise like scatterings of seed.
Church towers are distant, mark this territory
of those who've gone or those who never were —
churches in fields, no congregation near,
mere landmarks telling us where we are.
At night we moor beneath the stars
of country brilliance ; no landward lights
but those of nearby pub, blurred distant music
and raucous laughter, tinkling of a dry piano
as a door shuts and opens, people come and go,
and cars creep off like thieves along a secret road.
At last the lapping of quiet water,
a plop of otter underneath the bank,
spirals of fish-circles, and a hare
screams out three fields away, with bark of fox
and sounds that wonder us awake.
Only the calculating moon
looks down on all with pale indifference
inviting us to walk on water.

High-sided, narrow, the round-shouldered bridge
slopes steeply up for the sure-footed,
arches its humpback above the Kennett stream ...

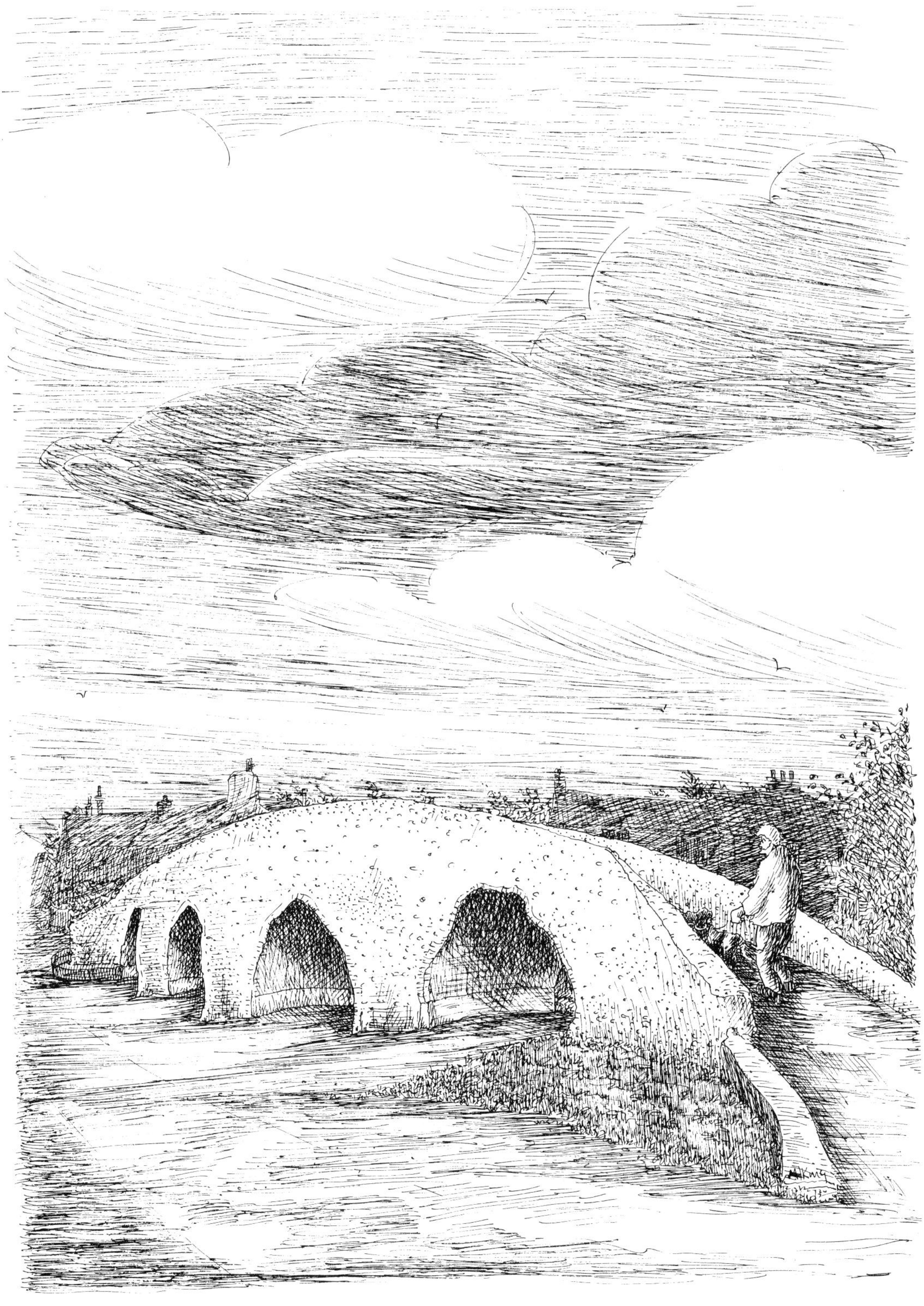

XIX PACK-HORSE BRIDGE, MOULTON

High-sided, narrow, the round-shouldered bridge
slopes steeply up for the sure-footed,
arches its humpback above the Kennett stream,
a dessicated summer river
trickling through reed-beds.   Five hundred years
it's stood here carrying the road
from Bury St. Edmunds on to Cambridge,
the one I would have walked from grammar school
to university if I'd been born
two hundred years before my time.
Imagine a student laden down with books,
feet blistered, dragging in the dust,
wishing he'd crossed a distant line of hills :
envious of wealthy friends who owned horses
whose height gave mounted views, peering over hedges
at longstrip fields, small colour-patch of crops,
bright summer's pasture-green against the brown
of fallow autumn harvested, they'd ride
along a wandering route that dived down sunken lanes,
grass tracks for cattle drovers and their herds —
whipcracks and shouts among the rising dust
announce with snort and bellow their approach
like children charging blindly out of school.
Then those on foot would jump into the ditch,
horsemen leap off or rein in hard
struggling to control their rearing mounts.
All would be glad to reach the bridge
where evil cannot cross the water.
Today's pedestrians, inquisitive
with cameras poised, guide books and maps in hand
fluttering like flags upon the parapet,
still cross this bridge that overlooks the ford
where cars pass through without a splash ;
superior feet are tracking history.

The sudden winter floods revive its use
except for cars whose drivers grumble at
a short detour. Sunshafts today on ochre stones ;
these buttresses were there before
King's College Chapel's ; at arch's centering
St. Edmund's Abbey stood entire.
No doubt some pilgrims paused upon this bridge
in make-believe that they were crossing Jordan
before King Henry's slighting of the shrines,
before in modern times new roads to Walsingham.

... behind the Priory's high altar site
is all that's left, the farthest eastern wall
where the great window collapsed into an arch,
the open space a tracery of feathery branches
of trees beyond the lawns, beating against the sky,
perspectives beckoning to eternity.

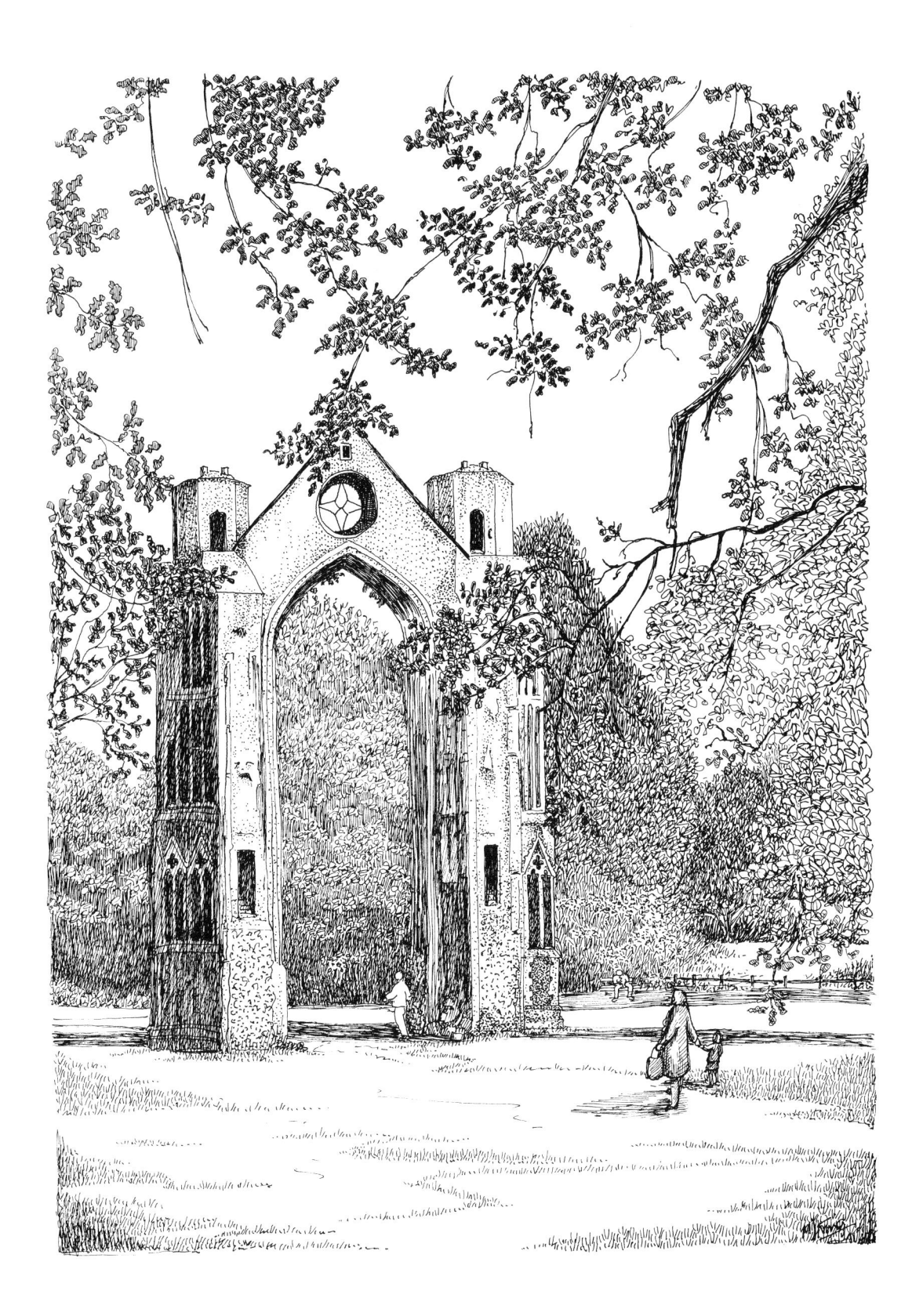

XX PILGRIMS TO WALSINGHAM

Therefore blessed lady, grant thou thy great grace
To all that thee devotedly visit in this place
     Richard Pynson, from a verse history of Walsingham, 1496.

You know how it is with pilgrimages :
you think you've got it planned —
staying with friends, not too far away
from the place you want to visit —
should give you a head, or rather more
than a foot start? Not all that business
of foot-slogging it from miles away,
taking a rucksack and a tent, camping out
in unfamiliar fields and, walking on your own,
there's no knowing what strange companions
you might meet up with on the way.
Then your map : ordinance survey, perhaps
not quite up to date — a footpath gone to ground —
afterwards it drops out of your pack somewhere,
getting you lost — or a sudden gust tears it
across the very place you're looking for.
It doesn't tell you where the best inns are
or farmers welcome campers in their fields.
All this is the hard work of prose
when you have poetry in your head,
the vision that draws you onward.

Every time I stayed with friends
living some thirty miles away at most
they'd say, *We'll go. We'll make it Friday.*
When I arrived on Thursday, though,
something else had turned up. *Next year,* they said.
So it went on, year by year. Pilgrim in my head
but not my feet, in someone else's car.
To go off on my own would be discourtesy.
They'd been so many times, described it all,
familiar with every detail :
how behind the Priory's high altar site
is all that's left, the farthest eastern wall
where the great window collapsed into an arch,

the open space a tracery of feathery branches
of trees beyond the lawns, beating against the sky,
perspectives beckoning to eternity.
Grant us true peace beyond this holy place.
Through the great arch where branches interlace
tree-shadows recompose a human face.
Imagination fills the nearer empty space
with the long nave of the Priory church
two hundred and forty four feet razed flat
but half the length of Ely. I'd read about
the vision of Our Lady appearing
before Richelde de Faverches,
lady of the manor, Little Walsingham,
more than nine hundred years ago,
not once but several times, instructing her
to build a replica of the house in Nazareth
to which the Angel of the Annunciation came.
The rest is history. From one act of faith
the Augustinian Priory rose
and many pilgrims' chapels on the way.
King Henry had the shrine and Priory destroyed
but faith goes on inhabiting a place.
This century the shrine, rebuilt
in ornate Baroque brick, the guide book states,
attracts a multitude of pilgrims once again,
and so religious faith regenerates a site.

One day I'll make it, and perhaps
remake a lapsed faith too, as one
apologist who makes confession.
Better to believe without having seen,
remembering St. Thomas and Our Lord.
Help, then, O Lord, all pilgrims' unbelief.
Give me the power to visualize,
to write about a place I haven't seen —
a paradigm of faith among the worldly-wise.

These poems' pilgrimage now has run
its course through twenty sites from Ely on,
link start and ending in religion,
where end may be beginning, and beginning end :
my winding road to Walsingham.

NOTES ON THE POEMS

I : Ely Cathedral : The Voyage Out

My sequence may be interpreted as a kind of pilgrimage, very indirectly from Ely to Walsingham. Theological rivalry between Ely and Cambridge in mediaeval times is referred to in this poem : in modern times the University maintains a boat-house on the river here — thus my reference to "the training crew".

II : A Postcard from Blakeney

On the North Norfolk coast the tide seems to go out forever, and the many small harbours are struggling against becoming silted up. Thus tourism in this area, attracting in particular wild-life enthusiasts, has superseded fishing. Blakeney's characteristic houses are of cobbles and flint.

III : Seacoast South of Southwold

Dunwich's decline from mediaeval times through coastal erosion promoted rivalry between Walberswick, Blythburgh and Southwold, with Southwold achieving dominance eventually. Parts of St. Andrew's Church at Walberswick were dismantled in 1695 in acknowledgement of that town's decline in its turn. A similar instance of a smaller, later, inner church replacing a larger, ruinous one (as at Walberswick) can be found at Covehithe, a decayed fishing port four miles north of Southwold.

IV : Upon Ickworth House

There have been Herveys living at Ickworth since 1485. The 4th Earl of Bristol, Frederick Augustus Hervey (1730-1803), also Bishop of Derry, began the present house in 1795. The architect was Francis Sandys. An enthusiastic continental traveller and collector of fine art, the Earl-Bishop intended Ickworth House to display his recent acquisitions, but these never reached England, having been seized by Napoleon in Italy in 1798. After the 4th Earl's death, his son was created Marquess; he completed the east wing of the house and moved in in 1830. In 1956, on the death of the 4th Marquess, the house and park were taken over by the Government in lieu of death duties and later given to the National Trust. The property now comprises house, furniture, paintings, sculpture, with shop and tea-rooms, as well as delightful gardens, extensive surrounding woodland (the Albana Walk) and parkland, all open to the public. The house is dominated by its striking rotunda and dome. A local tradition alleges that one of the marquesses of Bristol disguised himself as a gardener to avoid visitors, especially the uninvited and inquisitive general public. In my poem, his disguised appearance is conjectural and the conversation piece I have inserted is humorously fictitious.

V : Revisiting the Old School

Founded in 1550, King Edward VI School has occupied four sites in Bury St. Edmunds. It was in Eastgate Street until 1665, in Northgate Street until 1883, and then at the Vinefields overlooking the Abbey gardens and ruins until 1972 when part of it became St. James's Middle School. Part was demolished, and the rest — the Headmaster's house — was redeveloped into flats, the new comprehensive school taking over the Silver Jubilee School site. The loss of the Honours Boards during the demolition work was most regrettable, the World War I tablet being retrieved only through the vigilance of the caretaker. When writing the poem, I mistakenly believed that the Founder's Bust had also been destroyed, but David Weston, editor of *The Old Burian,* subsequently informed me that it was saved and moved to the King Edward VI Upper School's premises in Grove Road, the site of the former Silver Jubilee School. Miriam King's illustration was based on an old photograph of the main building before its partial demolition. The dormitory wing with its dormer windows has entirely disappeared, together with the staircase tower with the Foreigners' (boarders') entrance door giving access from the tarmac playground.

VI : St. Mary's, Dalham : Easter and Other Offerings

This poem explores relationships — between landed gentry and church, and between the gentry and their servants. Church and house stand close together, with the villagers living down below in the narrow valley of the Kennett. Comparisons are also made between the great storm that blew down the church spire on the 3rd September, 1658 — the night of Cromwell's death — and the hurricane of the 16th October, 1987, that brought down so many parkland trees here. Also mentioned are some unusual occurrences in the church itself in recent years.

VII : Wool-Gathering at Lavenham

This enormous church was endowed by wealthy wool-merchants, probably to salve their profiteering consciences. The town's population has increased very little since mediaeval times when, thanks to the wool trade, East Anglia vied with the Thames Valley as the most populous region of England. However, industry might have increased Lavenham's population in late Victorian times, but the first sugar-beet refinery to be built in England closed down through strikes and was converted into a hotel. Eventually the railway branch line was closed and the town reverted to its previously rather somnolent existence.

VIII : Bird's Eye View, Wicken Fen

Wicken Fen is a National Trust-owned bird sanctuary not far from Soham and on the southern edge of the Fens. It boasts a restored windmill and an exhibition centre displaying information about the local flora and fauna, especially bird-life, as well as accounts of traditional crafts such as thatching with the local reeds. The visitor can walk round the more marshy areas on raised duck-boards and there are several "hides" in the form of observation towers from which one can observe the bird-life and enjoy spectacular views of Wicken Fen and the surrounding countryside.

IX : Dunwich : the Last Survivor

Dunwich, now no longer in existence, was, in mediaeval times, the largest port on this part of the coast, but the silting up of the harbour and successive storms, which washed away the town and then attacked the cliffs behind it, wiped it off the map. On this cliff-top stood the last surviving church, All Saints, where, until recently and at the time I wrote this poem, only one tombstone survived, close to the churchyard's entrance arch. However, to save it from the rapidly advancing sea, John Brinkley Easey's stone has now been moved to the safety of Dunwich Village Museum. The skull on the beach is my invention. In the poem I have used "falanges" as more metrical than "metatarsus" — i.e. finger rather than toe bones, though the latter would have disappeared first ("going out feet first").

X : On the West Front, St. Edmundsbury Abbey

Recently proposals have been put forward to remove the houses incorporated into the ruined fabric of the West Front of the Abbey ruins some two hundred and fifty years ago. As a schoolboy, I was told about a ghost that would walk the gardens behind the houses, but my account has been fictionalised somewhat. A more common version of the story of the Grey Lady or Grey Nun claims that she scattered poison, while he was asleep, on the "Good" Duke Humphrey, founder of the Bodleian Library at Oxford University — this murder being committed in St. Saviour's Hospital, the ruins of which can still be seen in Northgate Street, near Bury St. Edmunds's railway station, far away from the Abbey buildings through which she is said to walk. The Abbey was probably the largest in England, and the design of the West Front with a central tower and two transepts is not repeated anywhere else except at Ely Cathedral.

XI : Grimes Graves

These are not "graves" but bell-pits from which flint was mined by neolithic man initially about 4,000 years ago. An iron ladder enables the public to descend over 30 feet into a pit that has been preserved. With some 360 or so excavations in close proximity to each other, these partially filled-in pits give the landscape a pock-marked appearance. The high quality flint mined here was used for implements such as axe-heads. An exhibition hut and shop is on this English Heritage site, and the custodian will accompany visitors down the ladder into the above-mentioned pit.

XII : Field Day on Cavenham Heath

This poem describes an incident that occurred during a King Edward VI School Junior Cadet Corps Field Day in the Breckland in 1943. Our uniforms bore a striking resemblance to those of World War I and thus inspired the deliberate echoes of Owen and Sassoon in the poem! Henry Reed's poetry collection, *A Map of Verona* (1946) became well-known for its "Lessons of the War" sequence—*viz*. "Naming of Parts", "Judging Distances" and "Unarmed Combat". In these three poems, the first of two contrasted narrators is the sergeant-instructor, a humorous source of stereotyped military terminology, while the second is the poet himself, a reluctant wartime soldier.

XIII : Gipsy Boy's Grave, Newmarket

The grave is beside a crossroads on the Newmarket-Bury St. Edmunds road just outside the village of Kentford, some two miles east of Newmarket. Folk-tales abound on the reason for and manner of this shepherd boy's suicide. Whether it was because he had lost a sheep, or dogs or wolves killed some of them, or he stole sheep belonging to someone else, the result was that he hanged himself rather than face the likelihood of the harsh sentences of early nineteenth-century courts — hanging or transportation to the colonies. In my poem, I have embroidered a less popular version of the story, in which his death was caused by unrequited love, its instrument a shot-gun. In one version of the sheep story, the missing sheep was found after he had killed himself. What is held to be true by everyone, however, is that those who leave flowers on his grave have remarkable luck at Newmarket's race meetings — but they mustn't be seen doing it!

XIV : Harvest Evensong at Gazeley

Here, an empty Victorian rectory has been superseded by a similarly empty, but much smaller, modern rectory — their shuttered windows staring at each other. A friend, a lay reader, took this service, in which the large church did not seem so empty with over a hundred parishioners attending and participating with great enthusiasm. No doubt the new rectory welcomed the new incumbent not long afterwards.

XV : On Newmarket Heath

The vast expanse of the Heath overlooks Newmarket from the east, providing marvellous all-round views. King Charles II was an early racing enthusiast, but his Court would bet on anything — witness Pepys's betting slips among his memorabilia, diary and books in the famous library that bears his name at his old Cambridge college, Magdalene.

XVI : Sunlight on The Backs, Cambridge

The Backs are so named because a large number of Cambridge colleges back on to them — an expanse of lawns, trees and gardens borders the Cam's left bank, with the backs of the colleges on the right bank. However, St. John's breaks this rule by its fourth court, New Court, having been erected on the left bank, and being joined to the rest of the college by the Neo-Gothic and un-Venetian Bridge of Sighs. When seen from a distance, the New Court looks like a wedding cake (thus its local nick-name) and recalls, in its architecture, Beckford's

Fonthill Abbey. At Fonthill, the elements of sun and frost loosened incorrectly mixed mortar so that the gigantic jerry-built tower collapsed, bringing down most of the rest of the Abbey with it. William Beckford (1759-1844) squandered his entire fortune on this white elephant of a Neo-Gothic building, little of which still stands today. In Cambridge, behind the New Court of St. John's, and entirely on the left bank, is Magdalene College and the Pepys Library which houses the famous Diary.

XVII : Turf Maze, Saffron Walden

Labyrinths of stone one hears of more in ancient history, but in Britain hedge mazes are much more common than turf ones. Turf mazes, open and flat, are frequently trod for wagers, according to folkloristic research. They also served as a learning pattern, probably representing spatial and directional relationships —you could call them precursors of maps! This theory is developed in "English Turf Mazes, Troy, and the Labyrinth" in *Folklore, Vol. 102, 1,* (1991) by Professor W.M.S. Russell and Dr. Claire Russell. Saffron Walden's maze was restored at frequent intervals in the nineteenth century and most recently in 1915. It is situated in the south-east corner of the Common.

XVIII : Not Far Off Breydon Water

Probably the largest expanse of open water on the Broads, Breydon Water is fed by the rivers Yare and Waveney. It runs inland from Yarmouth towards Burgh Castle, a large Roman fort of flint construction with massive walls 15 feet high and 11 feet wide at their base still standing on three sides.

XIX : Pack-Horse Bridge, Moulton

This fourteenth-century bridge still carries pedestrians over the River Kennett on what was the mediaeval Bury St. Edmunds to Cambridge road. Less than a hundred yards south of the bridge, a ford carries today's traffic across the frequently dried-up river-bed of the Kennett which, nevertheless, is occasionally subject to flash-floods.

XX : Pilgrims to Walsingham

In a thrice-repeated vision early in the twelfth century, the Virgin Mary showed the Lady of the Manor of Little Walsingham, Richelde de Faverches, the little house in Nazareth where the boy Jesus was brought up, and desired her to recreate it in Norfolk. This she did, building a stone church around the wooden house. In Edward III's reign, the Augustinians gained custody of the site and built a priory on it. As a place of pilgrimage, it rivalled St. Thomas à Becket's shrine in Canterbury Cathedral. However, at Henry VIII's Dissolution, the shrine and the priory were destroyed. It was not until 1931 that some Anglo-Catholics started building a replica of the mediaeval Holy House. Once again, Little Walsingham became a place of pilgrimage, as if the spiritual force of the place could not be suppressed by man. This poem symbolises an act of faith, in that this is the only one of my twenty sites that I have not visited, an example of unfulfilled intention, of a personal pilgrimage still to be achieved. And at a deeper level, it is also faith — religious faith — that I am searching for. Perhaps it is this underlying theme that provides some kind of unity to my sequence.